Dirty and Wet

by Michèle Dufresne

Contents

Pioneer Valley Educational Press, Inc.

Chapter 1
Spring

Bella looked out the window.

"Look, Rosie," she said.

"The sun is shining,

and the snow is melting.

I think spring is finally here!

Let's go outside and play."

Rosie looked worried.

"It's wet and muddy outside.

We might get dirty!" she said.

Bella nudged Rosie
towards the door.

"Come on, Rosie," said Bella.

"It will be fun."

It was a warm and sunny day.
Most of the snow had finally
melted away.
Rosie sniffed the air.
Bella sniffed the air.

"I love spring," said Bella.

"Me, too!" said Rosie.

Together the two small dogs
ran up the driveway.

When they came to the end of the driveway, Rosie turned around to go back home.

"Come on," said Bella.
"Let's go into the woods."

Rosie looked across the road towards the woods.
She looked very worried.
"Oh, no," she said.
"I get scared in the woods."

"Oh, Rosie, there isn't anything to be scared of in the woods!"

"You are so brave," said Rosie.
"But I get scared."

"I will take care of you," said Bella.

Rosie looked across the road towards the woods.

"It is wet in the woods," she said.

"We might get wet and dirty."

"We are dogs, Rosie.

Dogs *like* to get wet and dirty.

Come on, we are going into the woods."

She nudged Rosie across the road towards the woods.

Chapter 2
The Woods

Rosie and Bella set off down a path into the woods.

They stopped to smell everything along the way.

They smelled the bushes and the leaves.

They smelled the tree trunks and all the new things growing in the woods.

Then they listened to the bull frogs
in the pond and the birds singing
up in the trees.
Soon Rosie forgot about being scared.

All of a sudden, a squirrel came running through the woods.

"Woof, woof," barked Bella.

She chased the squirrel up a tree.

"Forget that squirrel," said Rosie.

"He isn't going to come down while you're waiting for him.

Let's go!"

"Look at this huge rock," said Bella.
Bella and Rosie climbed on the rock and
looked around.

"Oh! I see a big puddle," said Bella.
"Come on, Rosie!"

Bella ran and splashed in the puddle.

"Oh, this is fun!" she exclaimed.

"Jump in!" she called to Rosie.

"The water is cool and refreshing!"

"Oh, dear," said Rosie.

"You are getting wet!

You are getting dirty!"

"I am a dog.

Dogs *like* getting wet!

Dogs *like* getting dirty!"

Bella said.

"Oh, dear," said Rosie. "Oh, dear!"

Bella jumped into
another huge puddle.
The puddle was deep and cool.
"This is so refreshing.
Oh, I really like springtime!
Come on, Rosie.
This is so much fun."

Rosie watched Bella jumping around
in the huge puddle.
It did look like fun.
In jumped Rosie.
"Oh, dear! Oh, dear!" said Rosie.
"We are getting wet!
We are getting dirty!"

"This is wonderful!" said Bella.

Chapter 3
The Mud

After Bella and Rosie
finished jumping in the water,
they rolled in the mud.
"Oh, this mud feels terrific,"
said Bella.

"It does feel terrific," said Rosie,
"but we are getting very dirty!"

"We are dogs," said Bella,
"and dogs *like* getting wet and dirty!
Isn't this fun?"

Finally the two small dogs
turned around and started for home.
"Wasn't it a wonderful walk?" asked Bella.
"I'm so glad it's spring."

"Don't you think we look a little dirty?"
asked Rosie.

"Oh, Rosie, we aren't dirty,"
answered Bella.
"Just a little wet.
Wasn't it fun?"

"No!" said Rosie.

"It was not fun.

It was not fun getting wet and dirty."